I0442008

The Beautiful Stories

Of

The Great Seaport

Book 3

This book is the third in a series called *The Beautiful Stories of the Great Seaport.*

The collection of all the books in this series is separately published in one book as *Short Stories of the Great Seaport* **by the same Arthur**.

The Great Seaport Stories

THREE

Dedication

This book is lovingly dedicated to my nephews Chris and Peter, in recognition of their love of learning and their fascination with good, enlightening Short Stories.

THE GREAT SEAPORT STORIES

....SHORT STORIES FOR
RECREATIONAL READING.

....SHORT STORIES FOR
COMPREHENSION LESSONS,

....ESSAYS, PROJECTS,
WORKSHEETS AND ACTIVITIES

Prelude

In writing one more of this series of books, I am continuing with the joyful duty of conveying one of my own distinct ways of opening my eyes to see, instead of shutting them and pretending not to see my community, and the riches of our land. I would like to continue every endeavor that grants me the avenue to open my eyes wider in appreciation of others and the varied expressions of their values through their daily jobs and conscientious activities. These represent amongst other things, some noble pathways which provide due credit and grant worthy credence to people's worthwhile endeavors, their heartfelt devotions and sincere efforts to contribute to the richness of life, in whatever meaningful ways they are capable of, and with whatever worthwhile investments they could afford.

There is a good expression that "no one is an island". If some people were to attempt to walk through life closing their eyes, as it were, they would be definitely denying themselves the opportunity, the privilege and grand honor of connecting well with others. By so doing, they would perhaps inadvertently, be forfeiting the full appreciation and enjoyment of all the God-given beauty and glories that surround us.

Ranked high on the hierarchy of His divinely endowed riches rests the glories of God's human creation in all of its terrestrial grandeur and the inestimable celestial powers.

These speak of even greater dimensions of richness and substance that call for the depths of godly wisdom and inspiration, for the pristine revelation of that divine inner being which transients the ephemeral, and for the substantive sublime treasure which outlasts the transitory and reaches for the depths of the truest meanings of life. These congruently speak in favor of the inestimable gift of ultimate salvation and the fulfillment of that divine entity of immortality within of the souls of men.

Accessing and appreciating the unfathomable riches with which heaven has endowed all the beautiful lands and the blessed creatures who dwell in them, constitute a huge portion of the very essence of living, and of enjoying and sharing the fullness of the life which the ALMIGHTY God has granted unto each one of us here, as we prepare for the inevitable in the hereafter.

We shall do well then to live meaningfully in our own unique ways, while propelling ourselves forward towards the fullest actualization possible. Ultimately we do best by yielding centrally for the purpose of knowing our Creator with everything within our very existence, and committing ourselves totally to a lifetime of bringing Him praise and glory with everything we are and in all the things we do.

If you open your eyes to see, to obverse, to ponder and to share the best of who you are and what you are enabled by God's grace to do, you will invariably shine your light even in the darkest places and receive the enduring joys of helping to guide someone in the right path of life. You will surely bring calmness to a bothered or grieving soul and give a warm comforting embrace to someone in need, just when they need it the most.

You will encourage, and yes, you will bless someone by lifting a burden, even when you may not be aware of the full impact of your humble service, once you have heartily rendered it in the Lord's name. You will have calmed a trembling heart and wiped off a painful tear, when only God can see the strong, devout and noble heart behind your humble service; and you will never lose your reward from the Just Judge of this grand Universe.

Therefore, remain brave as you serve your fellow human beings, often doing so in the same way as you would serve your own brothers and sisters. Reach out and touch somebody with unselfish, pure, genuine love. When you yield yourself to do so in the Lord's name, you might happen to surprisingly find out that you become one of the most needed extensions of divine compassion and blessed grace, which historically uplifts people's souls from the crushing burdens of perilous earthly terrains to the godly comfort and exquisite conquering strengths associated with the blessed higher planes of Heaven's eternal riches encompassed with God's grace.

Therefore, humbly appropriate Heaven's grace for every needy hour, while you wholeheartedly yield yourself as the prepared instrument of God Almighty. Through you, *His Holy Healing Hands* touches the lives of His precious children with abundant goodness--oh what an unfathomable privilege, that'll be forever! Blessings to you!

Dr. Chrystolive Prince

****

Courage is contagious. When a brave man takes a stand, the spines of others are often stiffened.

Rev. *Billy Graham*

****

Preface

The world is spectacularly beautiful, its design is exquisite; the order and symmetry as closely constant in its organizational congruency with perfect loveliness, as the closely perfect arrangement of the classic symphony in an exceptionally illuminated symmetric orchestra. Christolive Prince

In his own words, Steve DeWitt in his outstanding book, *Eyes Wide Open: Enjoying God in Everything*, has said "Beauty was created by God for a purpose: to give us the experience of wonder. And wonder, in turn, is intended to lead us to the ultimate human expression and privilege: worship. Beauty is both a gift and a map. It is a gift to be enjoyed and a map to be followed back to the source of the beauty with praise and thanksgiving."

There are certain special geographical features in some regions of countries that distinguish them from other places. Each of those features brings to their region a distinct joy, an attraction and richness that becomes uniquely contributive to the overall blessings of the land. The United States of America is a land greatly endowed by the Lord God Almighty with many such striking and spectacular geographical landmarks. Some of these landmarks are the Seaports of the land.

In the selective *Beautiful Stories of the Great Seaport* as well as the collective *Short Stories of the Great Seaport,* we seek to discuss the features, activities and varied contributions of a major Seaport in the Pacific Northwest of the country. We explore the associated unique features of the Seaport, the daily activities as well as the distinctive roles it plays in the community and regional economy. In doing this, we are intentional in portraying its place as one of true significance to the overall dynamic living and operational functions of the entire society.

It is notably creative of the Arthur and pleasantly enlivening to have written these *Beautiful and well-crafted Short Stories of the Great Seaport as* presented, more as a historical non-fiction, while artistically incorporating many intriguing aspects to the narrative, without tampering with the documentary flow of the overarching message. The reader will hopefully, find the stories as truly enjoyable and in some places appropriately humorous without being unnecessarily satiric.

The *Beautiful Stories of The Great Seaport* and the corresponding larger collection of The Short *Stories of the Great Seaport* will hopefully challenge the young and the old alike to think more deliberatively in considering some related aspects of the inner workings of the democratic society portrayed. The considerations will equally tend to help us ponder on the subtle but challenging allusions to how we can all collaboratively help to build the society and make it work better for everyone.

The first parts of these book series have introduced us to the nature of the business of the Great Seaport and some of thrilling aspects of living near the water. We have equally deliberated on the subject of *containers* as an important equipment utilized in facilitating the job of loading and offloading the cargo at the Seaport. We shall proceed further in examining the subject of the importance of the *containers,* as well as the nature and use of the Seaport Terminals. As we do so, we hope to review the need for safe storage and the importance of adequate transportation in ensuring the efficient movement of those goods from the Seaport to their final destinations.

In subsequent books in these series we shall delve even further into some other stories about the types of recreational activities people engage in within the Seaport community. These stories encourage and celebrate different kinds of recreation, competitive sports and comradery, all of which are projected as major cultural ethos by the residents of the *Great Seaport* region.

Furthermore, this third book in the series of the *Beautiful Stories of the Great Seaport* is one which is highly recommended as a great text for self-learners and particularly for teachers and instructors of both k-12 and higher education. It is particularly excellent for teaching (or learning) various components of Language Arts including: Reading, Creative writing, and Composition, Vocabulary and

Comprehension. Many people will find them valuable instructional tools in literature, Geography, some History and titbits of Civics. Each of the segmented *short stories* is characteristically followed by no less than ten comprehension questions (with those of the fifth and sixth stories merged) for easy cross-referencing and compactible workability.

These comprehension questions are well designed not only to gauge the readers' level of understanding of the text, but also to further activate critical thinking, interactive deliberations on the various issues raised in the text, as well as creative writing, comprehension answers, accurate and precise summaries and short essays.

The *Short Stories of The Great Seaport* which specifically embodies a collection of all the stories and activities of the series, also incorporates the various interactive projects briefly explored in the selective series of the short stories. The suggested projects are carved to assist the interested reader further, in learning to internalize, demonstrate and practically apply some of the key lessons of the stories. The learners and instructors will find the nature of the suggested projects to be definitely engaging, encouraging the building of cooperative learning skills, and easily utilized for presenting positive steps towards the achievement of related career objectives.

These books will also serve as excellent resources for designing, planning and successfully executing productive field trips, particularly to a geographical landmark such as a Seaport.

Therefore, read the *Beautiful Stories of the Great Seaport* and the *Short Stories of the Great Seaport* as enjoyable recreational books or read them to learn more of the functions of a *Great Seaport*. You may study each as a textbook either as a strong text for various components of Language Arts or for some highlights in Geography, History, or titbits of related Civics.

As indicated, you may further use the books for better understanding or helpful resources for your field trips to some of the nation's Seaports, their nearby cities or regions, and in particular, to the *Great Seaport* region of the Pacific Northwest of the United States. For these purposes and a lot more, read these beautiful stories.

Additionally, the book, *Beautiful Stories of the Great Seaport* or the encompassing collective *Short Stories of The Great Seaport* will help you explore further, how the commercial activities of the busy and lucrative Seaports of your country, are closely intertwined with the prosperity and economic health of not only the specific regions where they are located, but also the overall wealth and economic health of the entire land. Enjoy reading, relaxing and incorporating the applications!

Dr. Chrystolive Prince

****

"God's beauty is the bouquet of His perfections in his person, unveiled in His purposes, and displayed in His Glory...Creation is beautiful, precisely because its Creator is beautiful. God defines beauty by His very essence. He is the source and standard of all beauty."

— **Steve DeWitt**, **Eyes Wide Open: Enjoying God in Everything**

The best and most beautiful things in the world cannot be seen or even touched - they must be felt with the heart.

Hellen Keller

Character is what a man is in the dark.

Dwight L. Moody

We are told to let our light shine, and if it does, we won't need to tell anybody it does. Lighthouses don't fire cannons to call attention to their shining - they just shine.

Dwight L. Moody

Jesus said,

Let your light so shine before men, that they

may see your good works, and glorify your

Father who is in heaven. (Math.5:16)

Holland America Amsterdam. Photo Courtesy of Don Wilson

THE JOURNEY OF THE CONTAINERS

We have had some good communication

about the purpose of containers and their

related importance to the efficient

operation and multi-dimensional functions

of the Great Seaport. The application of

containers has been established as

indisputably crucial, particularly in the

contribution of the Great Seaport to

regional, national and intercontinental commerce and overall economy.

We need to proceed with further deliberation on how the goods and general merchandise delivered through the containers actually get from the *Great Seaport* to their final destinations.

When the containers are taken off the ship by the container cranes at the dock, they are loaded into the trucks and transported to warehouses for storage. The *Great Seaport* has many large warehouses which hold all kinds of goods, from toys to refrigerators and motorcycles, to

mention but a few. These containers full of

goods are, of course, stored at the warehouses

temporarily as they must proceed quickly on

their journey to other designated places. The

highly organized Seaport operations not only

require but also ensure that the goods are

delivered on a timely basis, to the various final

destinations where they are usually awaited by

the consumers.

The goal of the Great Seaport management will remain to deliver the products and merchandise to the consumers in excellent condition. This reason often informs the decision to load certain goods directly onto trucks as soon as possible, after offloading them from the ships, and speed them off to the specified destinations for delivery. Whenever the scheduled delivery of goods involves perishable merchandize, additional caution is always implemented by the Port Authority, to ensure compliance with the exact set time frames scheduled for the delivery.

The schedules and general structure for delivery of merchandise as well as the associated enforcement mechanisms are both imposed and enforced by the predesignated appropriate sections of the administrative division of the Port management, for obvious reasons. The same objective for the preservation and efficient delivery of high quality goods and general merchandize, underscores the insistence on the appropriate provision of the Port's well-constructed warehouses.

Indisputably, the warehouses help to sustain the Seaport delivery capabilities much the same way as anchors serve the ships at harbor. They constitute a crucial segment of the overall functional infrastructure of the Great Seaport. The lofty goals of preservation and timely delivery of goods and merchandize in excellent condition also form major underlining reasons behind the stringent guidelines and requirements compelling proper security and high quality maintenance of the various warehouses of this notable Port.

The functions of the varied warehouses like other sections of the mega-administrative infrastructure of the Port, are not by any means carried out in isolation. Instead, they are upheld as integral portions which are intricately intertwined with many other crucial functional capabilities of the Seaport. While each division may hold a measure of distinct autonomy, their related duties understandably form indispensable pillars of the overall infrastructure. Therefore, the varied components of this multi-dimensional system are designed to function cohesively with high level operational efficiency in order to achieve optimal productivity in their service to the regional and national society. In guaranteeing the achievement of the anticipated outcomes of excellent transportation and delivery of goods and merchandize, the responsible officials of the notable Seaport with their myriads of dedicated workers, invest enormous time,

resources and efforts, to ensure the most

adequate and productive yields in quality

service to the people of the community and

the beloved Nation.

(Photo of container cranes moving cargo— courtesy of the *Port of Seattle*)

Rail Yard, Rail Cars and Truck Dispatchers

In addition to the convenience provided by the warehouses, the goods may also be carried to a rail yard or to a truck dispatcher center. Much of the cargo that is delivered through the *Great Seaport* is transported by railroad and by trucks to various parts of the country. The *Great Seaport* being located in the Pacific Northwest of the United States, has been noted to possess the capacity for delivering a large amount of cargo using this method of transportation, particularly to the Midwest and East coast of the United States.

The *Great Seaport* is also known for the record speed and efficiency with which it conducts the delivery of goods that arrive at the Port from different parts of the world. In order to facilitate the maintenance of this component of its functional efficiency, the Seaport ensures that many of the containers are quickly loaded directly onto trucks, soon after they are offloaded from the ships, from where they speed off to their final destinations.

Container Operations: Courtesy of the *Port of Seattle*

Additionally, a great deal of the containers are lifted onto rail cars for their journey. Many times containers are double stacked on rail cars which allows the trains to be able to carry a lot more cargo than they otherwise would. Sometimes, you may hear those who are running for public office, while contending for the citizens' votes, promise to expand truck lanes, build rail roads, and provide inter-state transits or some other forms of more effective transportation. This is because they usually understand how important these transportation services are to the citizenry, especially in relation to the efficient delivery of goods and

services to the consumers across the region and

beyond.

Electric Cranes-Rail Operations— Courtesy of D. Wilson, *Port of Seattle*

I am certain you will agree that effective transportation systems are crucial in every region and nation. The ability of people to safely and speedily utilize good transportation systems for themselves, as well as for the movement of material inventory and products, usually translate into the degree of entrepreneurial activities, creativity and economic growth of the particular region and surrounding suburbs . The extent of economic and other related avenues for healthy forms of lucrative social activity invariably equally influence the business climate of regional constituencies, while directly determining the level of employment

opportunities available to the residents.

When employment opportunities are plentiful,

the people can more easily take good care of

themselves and their loved ones. In addition,

they can afford to support their social and

charity orientated organizations for the good of

the general populace, and for the reduction of

social inequalities within the communities.

Noticeably, the environments marked by abundance of gainful employment and productive living enterprises tend to encourage a great deal of positive social events, in conjunction with significant devoted charity-oriented efforts by many who work collaboratively with their fellow residents, to enrich each other's lives in various ways. Under such heartening circumstances members of the communities are motivated to commit their concerted efforts and funds to provide much needed support and encouragement for their fellow citizens, particularly those who go through difficult circumstances and serious

privation.

Rail operations in the Union Pacific's ARGO yard,

Port of Seattle

When the vast majority of people are gainfully employed, they tend to be more occupied with issues related to their personal and cooperate productivity. The majority of those people tend to assume higher dimensions of personal responsibility for their own lives and usually would take more concerted positive actions to progressively develop their God-given talents.

While they are thus engaged in fulfilling, meaningful living, the people can be expected to demonstrate continued improvement in their abilities for sustaining high levels of personal quality living, as well as selfless commitment towards the welfare of others. Such high levels of personal growth, maturity and responsibility would usually be reflective in both the cooperate advancement of the outlook of the various local communities, and the cumulative contributive impact on the elevated standards of quality living for individuals and cooperate groups in the society.

Fortunately, when this is the case, there are multiplied resultant good effects easily noticeable in other aspects of the society. For instance, we can observe that instead of an increasingly disproportional percentage of the people's funds being invested by the community and the government in combatting crimes and maintaining prisons, a greater measure of valuable resources are committed towards good causes like improved education. By the same token, there will be larger amount of resources made available for investment in other uplifting societal institutions, as well the building of community infrastructure.

The people of the Great Seaport region understand and implement the foregoing deliberations, hence they take the building and maintenance of the varied transportation systems seriously. Consequently, their investments in the transportation systems in turn ensures that they continue to enjoy the wealth related benefits we have outlined.

Fortunately, the people also habitually and mercilessly tend to hold their politicians and legislators accountable, particularly for the campaign promises related to the delivery and maintenance of viable transportation systems in

the land.

Rail Operations, Union Pacific's ARGO yard, Port of Seattle.

Trucks with containers on SR-519, Photo by DON WILSON

Due to the importance attached to the issues related to efficient transportation systems, and the direct link with employment opportunities and the level of quality of living of the residents, the people tend not to take seriously any candidates running for public office who are unable to clearly demonstrate sufficient understanding in these matters.

Understandably, the people view candidates with a high level of understanding in this area of public service positively. At the same time, they usually would prefer that such theoretical understanding is also sufficiently coupled with

significant established record of job related

competence and accomplishments focused

mainly on the duties associated with the

political position being sought by the candidate.

We can respect the people's position that while

theory is important, nothing exactly replaces

actual industrial exposure and relevant

experience in the related areas, just as studying

a book on how to drive an automobile will not

necessarily translate into driving competence,

without the practical experience gained in

training on how to drive safely in the busy streets of the land.

Thus demonstrable capacity to deliver on the associated promises on the critical issue of regional transportation systems, when based more on experience than ordinary words, is often deemed more positively attractive to the citizenry. This is because the skills built into the knowledge with experience capacity, present more hope for the good of the land than mere eloquence or academic brilliant rhetoric.

After all said and done, very little else could effectively substitute for the facilitation of the efficient movement of people goods and services from one place to the other. Under such scenario, the importance cannot be overemphasized, of guaranteeing that the indispensable need for safe and efficient transfer of cargo from one place to the other is adequately met. Such adequate provisions enable the *Great Seaport* to effectively uphold the responsibility of timely, safe and efficient delivery of merchandize from the Port to their final destinations of the goods where

they are utilized by the people .

Container, Rail operations, Port *of Seattle*

Good Transportation and our Business

Obviously, the general public understands that ensuring efficient container operations or other forms of machinery for inter-city and inter-state delivery of goods, is an issue that must remain a top priority for any region or state, if they would continue to thrive economically. Efficient inter-regional or intra-continental transportation of goods, whether they are artistically created, agriculturally produced or otherwise manufactured, remains at the center of most business decisions.

Businesses small and great, are often intertwined in a number of ways with various other entrepreneurial personnel and enterprises, whose dealings with each other often involve the movement of products, people and services from one place to another. Consequently, they are usually involved in the transportation issues which directly impact the commercial climate of the cities and States

under which they operate at any given

time.

PHOTO—COURTESY OF WSDOT--**South Atlantic Street overpass visualization.** *The overpass, which opened in January 2014, allows freight and other traffic to bypass a busy train track.*

Rail Operations –courtesy --Don Wilson, Port of Seattle

Alaskan Viaduct

There has been a fierce debate in the Pacific
Northwestern State of Washington, regarding
the proposed replacement of the Alaskan Way
Viaduct in Seattle. The Viaduct which was a
huge transportation project completed in April
1953, is a double –deck elevated section of State
Route 99 which runs along the Elliot Bay water
front in the industrial district and downtown

Seattle. This major transportation route which carries over one hundred and ten thousand vehicles a day, was noted to have sustained some significant damages during the 2001 Nisqually Earthquake.

Subsequent semi-annual inspections have revealed continuing settlement damages to this key transportation route, giving rise to increased recommendations for the closure or replacement of the Viaduct. The proposed replacement was initially estimated to cost the Washington State Department of Transportation

(WSDOT) over 14 million dollars with the total cost of the project being about 4.25 billion dollars.

The Mayor of the city of Seattle during this time, had strongly argued that the projected estimate of the amount of money it will cost to replace the viaduct, will likely not be sufficient to cover the total expenditures associated with the replacement. The difference in estimated funds in such a case, would invariably be expected to leave the City of Seattle with the projection of an uncertain amount of money in cost overruns.

Eventually some of the contested issues in the matter led to a drive for a ballot referendum in 2011. Many major businesses in the region were noted for being in support of the Viaduct replacement project, including firms such as Microsoft and the Greater Seattle Chamber of Commerce. The result of the referendum, which was an approval of the project by a majority vote of the people, cleared the way for the viaduct rebuilding project to proceed. The boring of the project was therefore scheduled to begin in 2013 with the road way scheduled to open in 2015.

It is important to note though, that the Washington State department of transportation (WSDOT) began part of the larger project in 2008, while the replacement debate was still on-going, by repairing some of the viaduct columns.

The Viaduct replacement project was from the beginning anticipated to be a complex one, which gave rise to a rough organizational breakdown of some of the details of the sub-projects and expenditure associated with the overall construction and replacement. In this regard, the arrangements required that the City of Seattle would fund surface street improvements, utility relocation, and repairs to the Alaskan Way Seawall, which was also damaged in the 2001 Nisqually earthquake.

Moreover, Since the proposed tunnel would be expected to hold two lanes in each direction, as opposed to the Viaduct's three, resulting in the unavailability of the usual Western Avenue exit. Due to the fact this is the same exit which usually served the Belltown, Interbay, Magnolia and Ballard areas, King County would be expected to further provide the fund transit improvements to effectively offset the loss.

In addition, there has been an understandable expectation that *The Port of Seattle* would undertake funding part of the project as indicated in *SoDo.* Additional hundreds of millions of dollars for some of these and other associated projects will be realized from *tolls*, at rates set and enforced by the Washington State Transportation Commission.

Zone 1-- Railroad Way South to South Washington Street--
Courtesy of **WSDOT.**

Bertha began her tunnel drive at the south end of downtown below sea level. In this first stretch of tunneling, Bertha will dig under fill soil dumped here by Seattle's early settlers. Because the machine is shallow at this location, crews built underground concrete walls on either side of the tunnel route to hold the ground in place. They also built protected areas underground where Bertha will stop so crews can do planned inspections and maintenance before the machine dives beneath downtown Seattle.

Courtesy of WSDOT

&&&&&&&&&&&&&&&&&&&&&&&&&&&&&&&&&&&&

&&&&***

****

It is a masterpiece of the devil to make us believe that children cannot understand religion. Would Christ have made a child the standard of faith if He had known that it was not capable of understanding His words?

Dwight L. Moody

(((

(((

God's word eliminates the conscience enlightening the eyes to see.

They will grant full strength for the whole day, hope for the future and

The propelling thrust, all sufficient for, the entire journey.

Dr. Chrystolive Prince

Bertha

The Viaduct boring project was nicknamed "Bertha" after Bertha Knight Landes who was the first female Mayor of Seattle. The boring project commenced on July 2013 as anticipated and was expected to be completed in about fourteen months, though this schedule was soon interrupted by a number of unforeseen events.

First, there were some problems originating from the fiberglass near the front of the drill. This was soon additionally compounded by the labor disputes with local Union organization.

The Project was further delayed in December 2013 when the boring efforts struck a steel pipe, installed as a well-casing for an exploratory well drilled as part of the planning phases of the project. This second set of delays eventually lasted for more than two years, even as the project workers toiled hard to dig a 120-

foot (37 m) vertical shaft down to *Bertha's* cutting head to repair the breach. This huddle, in addition to the discovering of *Settling* around Pioneer Square, caused more extension of efforts and time in order to move the project expeditiously forward as originally planned.

Seattle Tunnel Partners Rotating Bertha's Cutterhead— WSDOT.

-- Seattle Tunnel Partners Rotating Bertha's Cutterhead

WSDOT Betha Operations —(December , 2015)

Trucks and Containers towards the Highways

Fortunately, the Tunnel boring was ultimately resumed on December2015. Currently, Seattle Tunnel Partners have projected their firm commitment to the cause, with expectations to have the tunnel completed and open to traffic in 2018. Notwithstanding, whereas the concerted extended efforts of rebuilding and modernizing the waterfront area will continue as expected to until 2019.

When the entire construction is completed, the decades old Battery Street Tunnel which has been another important transportation service route will also be

filled in and sealed. This is because the

Battery Street Tunnel is deemed old, and

the Tunnel no longer satisfactorily meets

the higher modern safety standards.

Therefore it has been determined that the

community is better served by not

continuing to carry the associated risks of

keeping it open.

 Inspite of the foregoing reason, the

Battery Street Tunnel is also quite

expensive to maintain, and will be made

redundant by the completion of the Alaskan Way tunnel anyway. Upon the completion of the entire project, all the dirt produced by tunnel construction will be sent to fill a *CalPortland quarry* which is located in Port Ludlow, Washington.

The Great Seaport region and other neighboring states of the Pacific Northwest envision increased lucrative economic activity and boom from the successful completion of the *Bertha* project and the entire Viaduct replacement. It is indisputable that there will be tremendous multi-dimensional benefits, which will continually flow for the long term, from the availability of those enhanced, reliable transportation routes.

The full range transportation services of the additional routes, will be in reality fully deployed and maximized as expected, upon the completion of the Alaska way Viaduct replacement. The level of this gain is elevated with the maximum advantage of fuller capacity services associated with the connectively of many other closely related transportation routes within the immediate vicinity and surrounding regions. This is emphasized by the availability and direct connection with key interstate highways for enhanced movement of people and cargo. The modernization and advancement of the major Alaskan Viaduct and the other noted transportation routes, bring forth much more promises of continued blessedness and realization of compounded increase to the cities of this beautiful city, and the entire surrounding regions of the Great Seaport.

In succeeding books in this series, we hope to discuss more contributions of the Great Seaport, along with the joyful activities of the residents of this remarkable region. It would be also important for us to take additional views of the interconnected operations of the famous Port with the partner WSDOT, which should include exploring the progressive building of the crucial *Bertha* project, as it journeys towards its completion and the anticipated grand opening.

****

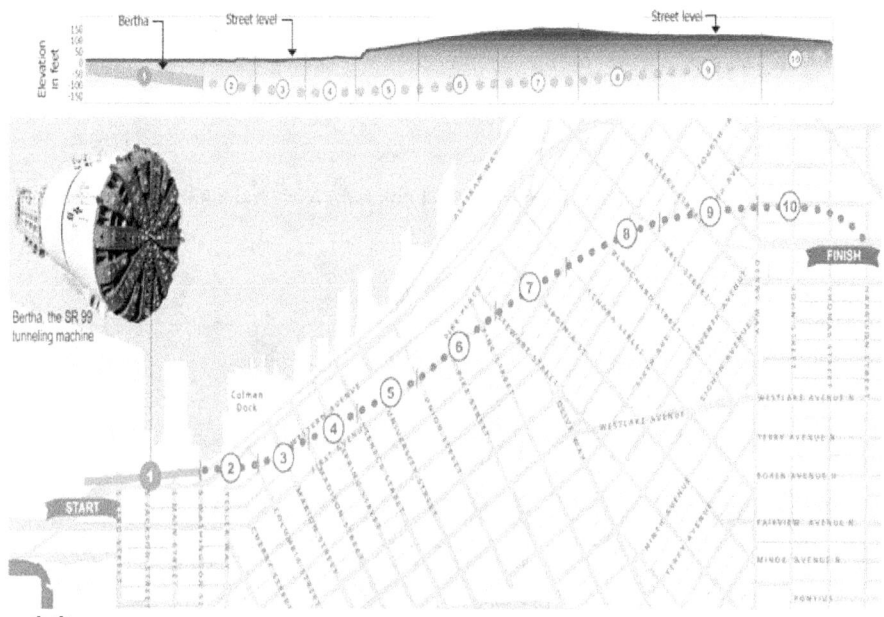

 In the immediate preceding picture it can be observed that the tunnel route has been divided into 10 zones. Each zone has something about it that makes it unique, such as a certain soil type or a noteworthy location beneath the city. The map shows the entire tunnel route. The machine is currently located *in zone 1 executing the*

projects and continually making progress as planned.

****

(A section of the Alaskan way Viaduct—Photo courtesy of the WSDOT)

** * * * * * ***************

COMPREHENSION QUESTIONS AND PROJECTS

* *

For the readers who intend to utilize these

stories for classroom instruction, the

following recommendations and projects

should be helpful. They could be even more

beneficial where the methodology applied

for specific ranges of instructional delivery

allows flexibility with varied instructional

tools, which are adaptive to the overall

curriculum.

In many cases the educator and other

facilitators of instruction, may also use the

following incorporated comprehension

questions as a template for short essays,

skill practice inferences, or in conjunction

with portions of the short story, for various

grammar component worksheets.

* *

In addition, the teacher or instructor

may utilize the content of the stories to

construct various cooperate learning

projects. For example, the students may

use construction sheets, cardboards,

paints and other materials to build their

own 'Great Seaport' complete with decks,

trucks and container terminals. They may

similarly design operational trucks and

trains and further discuss the importance of

these means of transportation in the

effective operation of the Great Seaport.

Furthermore, the learners will necessarily

relate specific operations of the Great

Seaport as demonstrated in these Short

Stories, to its varied contributive roles

towards the viability of the regional and

national economy. These activities and projects could easily translate into Short Essays --with themes centered on the operations of the Great Seaport and various other related subject matters. They could equally form the framework for competitive creative writing with presentations based on the various related subjects.

*The student writers benefit immensely when they are carefully guided to choose the topics of greatest interests to them, which might include aspects of the practical effects of major *"economic hubs"* like the Great Seaport, on the overall quality of life of the general citizenry in a given geographical region.

****

COMPREHENSION QUESTIONS AND PROJECTS CONTINUED

* Furthermore, the students should discuss their work in project teams (interspaced with reflective quizzes) and sequentially *incorporated with written summaries or*

project papers outlining their main

discoveries, findings and conclusions.

*These could be formally submitted with

some of the project demonstrations accrued

in class presentation sessions.

The students'/participants' papers,

presentations and class projects should be

assessed, graded, saved, and/or justifiably

rewarded as part of the learners' overall

participatory academic portfolio which

would be reflective on their final end

grades.

Viable incentivizing tools such as indicated

above, remain some of the most successfully

proven instruments of efficient cooperative

learning, the effective encoding of

important curricular concepts; usually

potent for strengthening retention and after

school knowledge transference, with long

lasting demonstrable impact in practicum

rewards.

88888888888888888888888888888888888*****

****

* *

FIELD TRIPS

* *

A field trip to a seaport will be a perfect

project to integrate into the series of lessons

centered on *The Great Seaport Short Stories.*

The Port of Seattle in the USA is particularly

noted for being very welcoming to students

across many grade levels for educational

visits to the Port. The Seaport staff will be

glad to offer a class to visiting students,

provided they are notified of the scheduled

trip ahead of time. The class will prove

immeasurably helpful in further educating

the students regarding some of the trade

activities of the Seaport. Such trips will

equally provide necessary practical

educational exposures to the upcoming

generation with respect to the many good

career opportunities the Seaport offers. In

addition, those who visit the Seaport would

likely have the opportunity of seeing first

hand in some demonstrable ways the types

of jobs that people do at the Port and gain

some measured insights into the details

involved in some of those lucrative jobs.

In order to be most integrative into the

learning process The field trip could need to

be followed up later(not necessarily the same day) with class discussions and 'summary of findings' compositions on the trip by the learners. Corresponding

Assessment of such sessions should preferably be guided to be on the lighter side, interactive and enjoyable, while investing sufficient concentration on building on the most possible engagement of the interests of the learners towards academic, social and other life skills advancements.

***Projects like the ones we discussed above are--- are excellent frameworks for class quizzes and essays.

In particular, when you are applying this aspect of learning assessment and evaluation with much younger students, the essays need not be sophisticated and lengthy. The most important thing is integrating the lessons in such a way as to

enhance the ability of students to grasp the

relevant concepts, interpret them correctly,

and demonstrate the understanding of how

to practically apply them in real life.

The class projects will be aimed at challenging the

students' creative skills; they will be particularly

geared towards strong learning opportunities,

building career objectives, as well as enhancing

the development of the students' cooperative

learning skills.

Comprehension Questions

1. Why do the trucks carrying containers loaded with the goods from ships need to *speed off* to their destinations'?

2. What will be the possible impact of any situations that significantly slows down the journey of the trucks and containers?

3. Why do you think those running for public office in various cities and states often emphasize transportation issues in their campaigns?

4. Specify the relationship between a good transportation system and the availability of jobs in a city or state?

5. How do you think *'the lucrative activities of the Great Seaport'* impacts the standard of living of the people in the region where it is situated?

6. How would you describe the relationship between good railroads and inter-state commerce?

7. How does fast and efficient container delivery affect the overall health of the people of the United States of America?

8. Describe how the *'journey of the containers'* helps to shape national political and economic initiatives?

9. How does the effective operation of the Great Seaport regional commerce, directly or indirectly impact the intra- continental commerce of the USA?

10. Could the successful operation of *the Great Seaport* affect your family if they do not live in the Pacific Northwest of the United States?

11. How do you think that the *Great Seaport* container delivery systems could contribute to a healthy economic climate in the world?

12. Why do you think may people considered it a good idea to name the viaduct replacement project "Bertha"?

13/14*Conduct a class /personal short reflective research project on the first female mayor of Seattle. Write a paper based on this research.

15. What do you consider to be her greatest contribution to the region she governed. Outline the different lessons we could all lessons can we learn from her legacy?

"When we experience a moment of beauty, we should turn wonder into worship by giving thanks to God for His goodness in providing it, for His creativity in making it, or simply for our pleasure in experiencing it...The greatest wonder is not the music itself but the Musician, not the creation but the Creator. He is beautiful."

Steve DeWitt's (*119, 9*)

Tears shed for self are tears of weakness, but

tears shed for others are a sign of strength.

Rev. Billy Graham

Bay Marina,Courtesy Port of Seattle: Don Wilson.

The next time you think of highly talented precious people who are richly blesssed by God Almighty, do not quickly count yourself out. You are precious to God too. Do your very utmost best to develop and apply whatever talents God has endowed you with (whether they seem great or small), for there will be an enriching harvest for you. wholeheartedly commit your entire life into God's hands and keep your whole trust in Him—Always.

Dr. Chrystolive Prince

****

++

The Almighty will defend Us!

Whatever comes tomorrow,

To the Army of Jehovah,

He'll Grant the Victory Shout!

CHRYSTOLIVE PRINCE.

Other Books by Dr. Chrystolive Prince

i.   **The Simple Fives**(Classic Inspirational Work--- (a series) *Also DOWNLOAD in Mp3 Audio files

ii. **Overcrowding** in Schools: *Confronting the Challenge)*

iii. *Beautiful Stories From The African (a series)*

iv.   Beautiful Stories of the Great

Seaport (a series)

v.**Short Stories of The Great Seaport: *short stories for recreation, comprehension lessons, worksheets, projects & activities,* by the same Author

✝ CHRYSTOLIVE PRINCE

Amazon.com and on *Createspace.com.* *Download and read---Kindle.com*

*888***

888**************88888888888888*****

****

****

This publication is a series

To be continued in The Beautiful Stories of the Great Seaport: Book FOUR

****Short Stories of The Great Seaport:**
short stories for recreation, comprehension lessons, worksheets, projects & activities, by the same Author **CHRYSTOLIVE PRINCE**

Amazon.com and on *Createspace.com.*
*Kindle.COM

* *

ACKNOWLEDGEMENT

I hereby express my appreciation of the *Port of Seattle,* for their encouragement and invaluable services to the Northwest Region of the USA, the Nation and the Globe. Many special thanks also to photographer Don Wilson and her team, of the Port of Seattle, for the courtesy of many of the excellent photographs. I also thank the

Washington State Department of Transportation (WSDOT) for their noted contribution.

References

1. THE HOLY BIBLE (KJV) *All scriptural references

2. Steve DeWitt's outstanding book, *Eyes Wide Open: Enjoying God in Everything*, Credo House, 2012. 119,9

3. **Chrystolive Prince**, **Short Stories of the Great Seaport.**

www.ingramcontent.com/pod-product-compliance
Lightning Source LLC
Chambersburg PA
CBHW072142280526
45788CB00002B/743